Helpful Tips for Coloring

- It's always a great idea to try your colored pencils, markers, gel pens on the Color Test Page first to ensure you're getting the color you're looking for.

- If you find that your marker or gel pen bleeds on the Color Test Page, put a scrap piece of paper behind the page you are coloring.

- Be sure to keep colored pencils sharp for those detail areas.

- Remember to slow down and take your time— the more you enjoy yourself, the happier you'll be with your drawings.

- Have FUN and color outside the lines...it's ok!

COLOR TEST PAGE

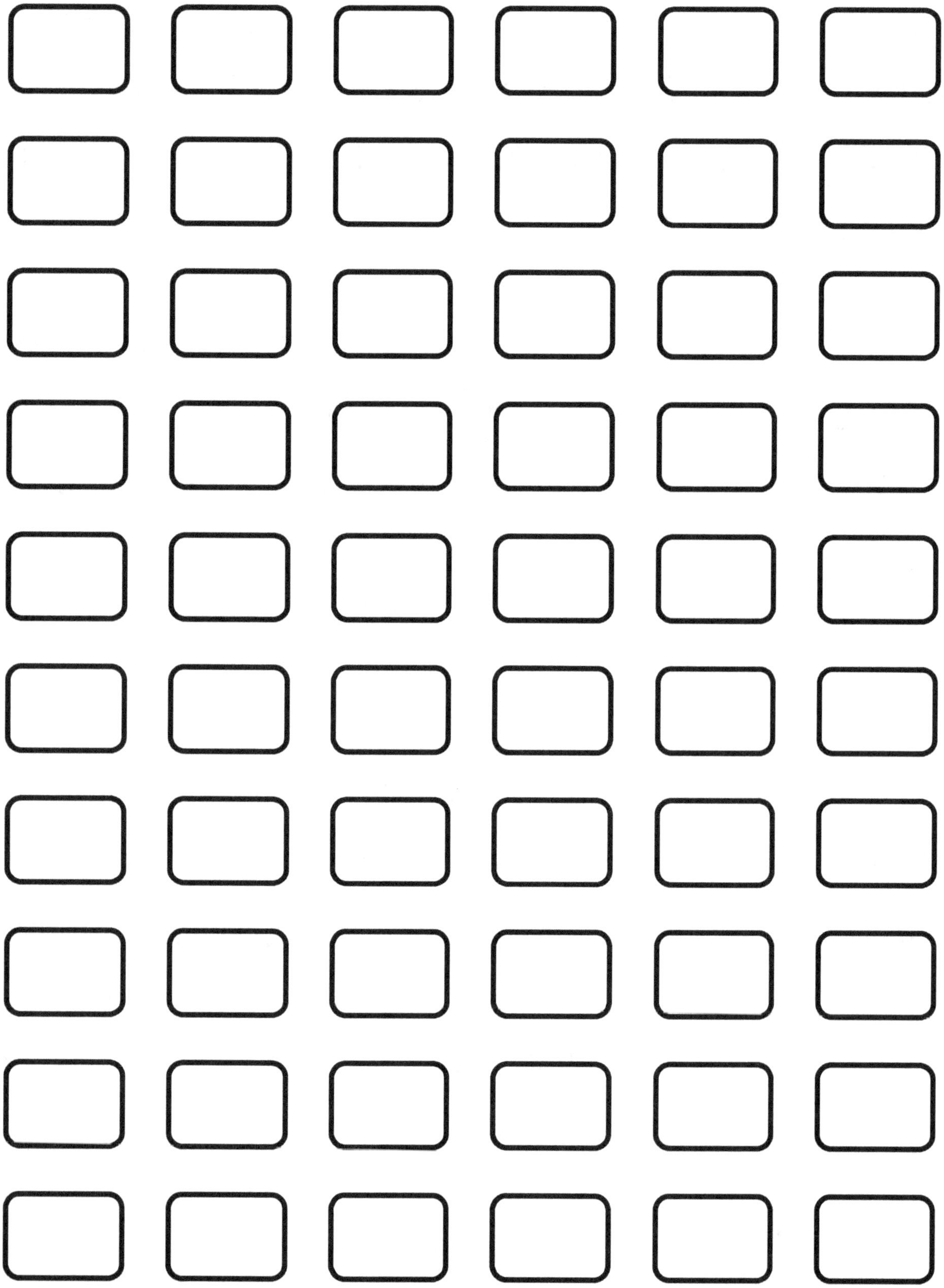

COLOR TEST PAGE

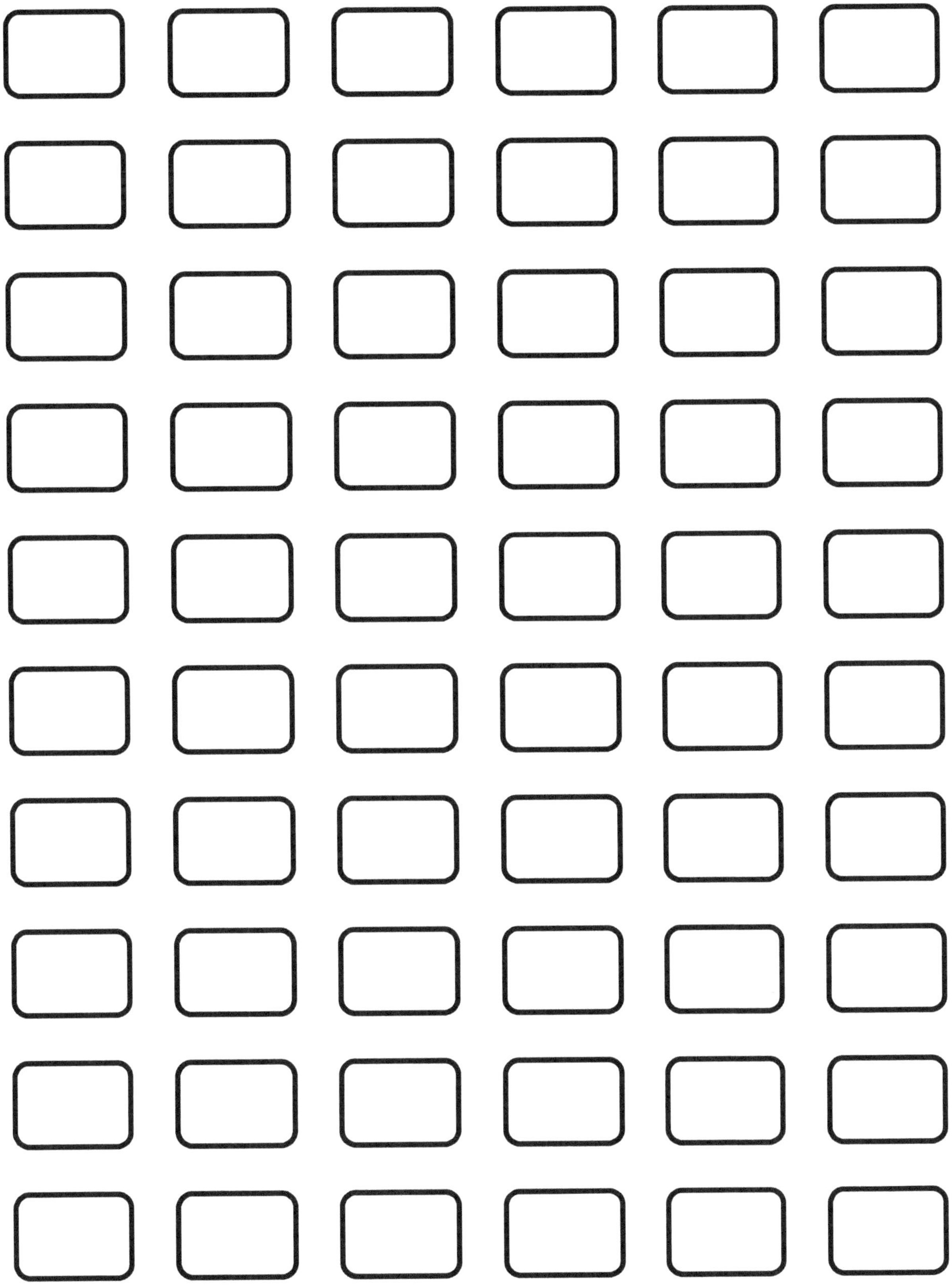

Thank you for choosing

COLOR THERAPY COLORING BOOKS!

We really appreciate your business and would love your feedback! Please share your thoughts on Amazon and add photos of your completed masterpieces!

www.ingramcontent.com/pod-product-compliance
Lightning Source LLC
Chambersburg PA
CBHW080046260726
48658CB00007B/2767